CLIP AND GROOM YOUR OWN POODLE

a simple, step-by-step illustrated course on clipping and grooming all types and sizes of poodle.

by WILLIAM LA FETRA

Acknowledgments

We thank all those people whose professional knowledge and long experience in clipping and grooming Poodles has been molded into this book. Thanks also to the photographers who supplied us with the excellent and informative photos, and to Ernest H. Hart for the drawings that enhance the text.

ISBN 0-87666-356-0

© 1972 by T.F.H. Publications, Inc., Ltd.

Distributed in the U.S.A. by T.F.H. Publications, Inc., 211 West Sylvania Avenue, P.O. Box 27, Neptune City, N.J. 07753; in England by T.F.H. (Gt. Britain) Ltd., 13 Nutley Lane, Reigate, Surrey; in Canada to the book store and library trade by Clarke, Irwin & Company, Clarwin House, 791 St. Clair Avenue West, Toronto 10, Ontario; in Canada to the pet trade by Rolf C. Hagen Ltd., 3225 Sartelon Street, Montreal 382, Quebec; in Southeast Asia by Y.W. Ong, 9 Lorong 36 Geylang, Singapore 14; in Australia and the south Pacific by Pet Imports Pty. Ltd., P.O. Box 149, Brookvale 2100, N.S.W., Australia. Published by T.F.H. Publications Inc. Ltd., The British Crown Colony of Hong Kong.

Foreword

IN EVERY country in the wide world, wherever a plane, auto, ship, train, camel or oxcart can take you, you will find that breed of dog known internationally as the Poodle. In all the many cute and useful clips (and their number is legion) to which the Poodle is heir you will find these wonderful dogs parading the streets of the far-flung centers of civilization of this earth. Somehow one feels that the Poodle is the canine personification of civilization and its fellow traveler, sophistication.

Certainly we Americans have taken the Poodle to our hearts, for the record of American Kennel Club registrations leaves no doubt that the Poodle is the most numerous breed of dog in this country . . . and by no small margin. In 1965 there were 207,393 individual Poodles registered by that august body in the United States, with the breed that is in second place, the German Shepherd, numerically far behind the Poodle with 78,241 being registered during the same time period.

There is no sign that this tremendous popularity will abate. As a matter of fact all indications point to still greater popularity in the future. It is no great wonder, under the circumstances, that grooming salons are constantly blossoming out all over the country, in pet shops, dog breeding establishments, veterinary hospitals, or as individual grooming and clipping centers. The cost of keeping a Poodle looking its best, as well as the time necessary to bring it to the dog-groomer and later pick it up, is considerable. Also, many owners would enjoy grooming and clipping their own dogs if they knew how to do it.

The purpose of this book now becomes obvious.

By following the illustrated and simply written directions implicitly and by indulging in a bit of patience and a lot of practice, the average Poodle owner can keep his pet looking well groomed and neat. If you have normal intelligence and can use your hands for normal tasks, you can clip and groom your own dog and do it well . . . provided you are given the correct information as to the tools you need and should buy, and a good book that enhances the written word with clear illustrations.

This is that kind of book.

Many people find that they have a flair for grooming and clipping, a special talent that makes the chore easy and enjoyable. Such individuals frequently become professionals in the field, opening their own grooming salons, or using the knowledge gained from this book to add to their total earnings by grooming and clipping as a pleasurable and profitable sideline.

You will probably make mistakes at the beginning. Luckily these mistakes will not be drastic so do not allow them to concern you to too great an extent. You will learn by your mistakes and, with the passage of a little time, the hair will grow back to cover your mistakes. Be patient, be calm, and practice diligently and your reward will be the immaculate and handsome appearance of your pet Poodle.

Contents

Foreword

1 **Your Poodle's Coat**   7

2 **Necessary Grooming Equipment**   9

3 **Brushing**   13

4 **Bathing and Drying**   15

5 **How to Clip Your Poodle**   21

6 **The Basic Clip**   28

7 **The Puppy Clip**   32

8 **The Show Clips**   34

9 **The Dutch Clip**   42

10 **The Lamb Clip**   46

11 **The Town and Country Clip**   50

12 **The Summer Clip**   52

13 **The Kennel Clip**   53

14 **Mustaches and Color Tinting**   56

15 **The Professional Dog Groomer**   58

16 **Mimic and Fun Clips**   62

The Poodle is one of the most appealing pets in the world. The many patterns in which his coat may be trimmed has also made him one of the most fashionable. For coat and skin health and so that your Poodle will look and feel his best, the grooming and clipping of his coat should have regular attention.

CHAPTER 1

Your Poodle's Coat

THE COAT of the Poodle has been the focal point of controversy for many years. A great many breeders have claimed, with absolute conviction, that the Poodle possesses a single coat with variance in the structure of each hair from the outer tip to the base or root. Other authorities just as vehemently declare that the Poodle has a double coat, in common with other canine breeds, consisting of an undercoat, or wooly, waterproof, protective base-coat, and an outer-coat, the so-called guard hair that is coarser, longer, and is the coat most obvious to the observer.

Scientists who have studied coat structure in the Poodle agree that the breed is double-coated and, since their analysis is clinical and precise, we can assume that their findings are correct. The Poodle, like other canines, sports a double coat.

It is true, however, that the nature and the quality of the Poodle's coat is rather unique and lends itself to varied handling and designs in clipping. It has the quality and appearance of Persian lamb; it is fine, fluffy, and light in texture and knots readily when not conscientiously cared for, much to the exasperation of the Poodle owner.

You will be informed by many owners and breeders that the Poodle does not shed its coat. This, too, is a fallacy. The Poodle sheds its hair just as does any other breed. But, the shed hair is caught and trapped by the undercoat and packs down. This shedding process is encouraged by owners and handlers of show dogs for it provides a strong base from which the sprouting, comparatively straight, fine guard hairs can gain support and stand out straight to form the familiar fluffy mane of the show Poodle wearing an English Saddle or Continental Clip.

Unfortunately, due to the fine quality and profuseness of the Poodle's coat, lack of frequent barbering quickly results in an odorous mess that makes the animal uncomfortable and objectionable both to itself and to those who live with it.

The Poodle coat in all its glory. The English Saddle show Clip modeled by two elegantly groomed Poodles.

A silver Miniature

A snowy white Toy

CHAPTER 2

Necessary Grooming Equipment

IN BUYING the grooming and clipping equipment you will use, the best will be the cheapest in the long run. A few extra dollars spent initially will give you many more years of trouble-free usage and will do the job better and with greater ease of handling, this latter reason is a pertinent one for the beginner.

Now, let us proceed to the tools you will need to work with. Select a table (a card table is a good height), box or crate on which to place your dog while you clip him. Be sure that the height of this platform will allow you to work with comfort and ease without undue bending. An arm, of metal preferably, or of wood, in the form of a reversed L should be fastened firmly to the clipping platform, the horizontal arm high enough to allow about a foot of space above the head of your Poodle when it stands on the platform. A light leash or chain attached to this overhead arm and fastened to the collar of your dog will help to hold and steady him leaving your hands free to perform their task. This "L" or "grooming stand" can be ordered from your pet shop. A rubber mat on the clipping table top will prevent the dog from slipping.

The most important item of necessary equipment is, of course,

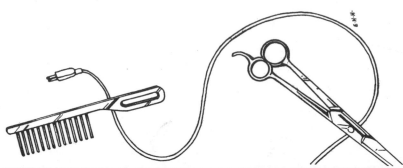

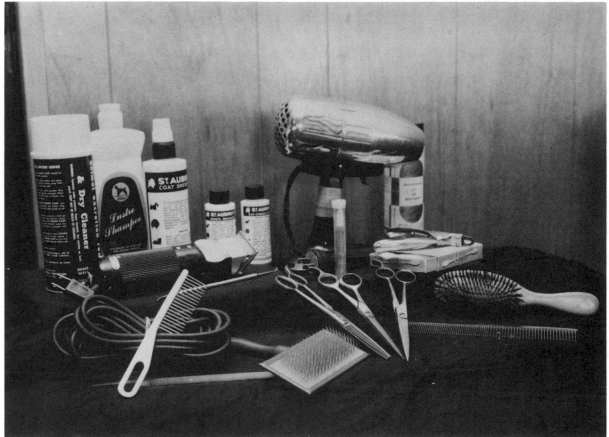

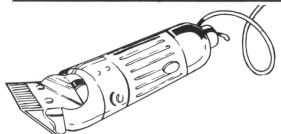

All the essentials necessary to groom and clip your Poodle properly are illustrated here. The better your equipment the longer it will last and give you trouble-free service.

the electric small animal hair clipper. There are several brands and prices can range from ten dollars to fifty dollars according to quality. There is even a set being marketed for human barbering containing a plastic clipper, shears, comb, etc., that is priced at under ten dollars. Kennel owners and professionals must necessarily have the best for nothing less would stand up under the constant use.

You should purchase a clipper with interchangeable heads so that you can, when you become expert, use blades of different sizes. Of the many brands in use the one that is perhaps most commonly utilized by veterinarians, kennel owners and professionals, is the Oster Small Animal Clipper.

Here is a list of all the essential grooming equipment.

1. An "Oster" (or comparable) clipper, with an extra head.
2. Clipper blades. Two each of No. 10, No. 15, No. 5, No. 7, No. 5/8 and No. 30, the No. 30 to be used only by a professional.
3. Electric Dryer. The Oster Co., manufacturer of the clipper recommended, also makes the Oster Airjet Dryer (recommended).
4. Wire brush, made for Poodle grooming.
5. Nail trimmer. "Resco" is a good one. Or you can purchase a toenail filing attachment that can be used on your electric clipper.
6. Steel-toothed comb, made for Poodle grooming. Half the teeth fine, half coarse.
7. Barber shears. Two pair. One straight, one with curved-end blade.
8. Tweezers or Hemostats. To pull hair from inside of ears. Must be used with caution.
9. Shampoo, made for Poodles (tearless kind if possible). Ear powder. Benzyl Benzoate. Coat dressing. Boric acid powder. Mineral oil. Medicinal cotton.

The Oster Clipper is the finest small animal clipper made. Get the A–2 or A–5 model, the latter boasts a detachable blade feature that makes changing blades quicker and easier. Boric acid powder soothes if hair must be tweezered from inside the ears. The ear powder should be medicated and useful in keeping the ears free from canker or other infection. Benzyl benzoate, is effective in preventing dry skin and protecting against exterior parasites, when it is mixed with the shampoo. The coat dressing gives a beautiful sheen and finish to the coat. Mineral oil can be put into the dog's eyes as a protection against the burn of the shampoo unless the shampoo used is "tearless."

For the best results make sure that you work in comfort, using a grooming table of the correct height.

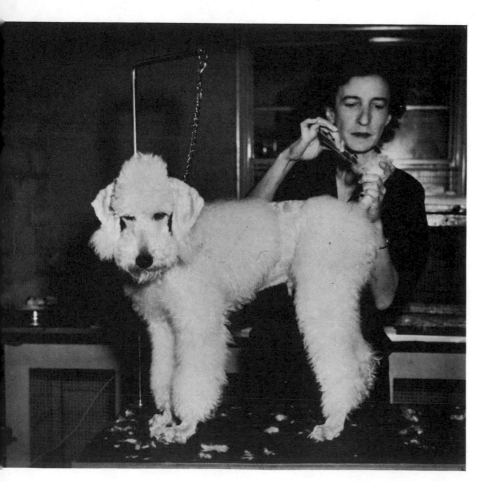

A professional grooming table of metal with a rubber surface mat and an adjustable grooming arm.

CHAPTER 3
Brushing

BRUSH YOUR dog before you bathe him. This is, of course, contrary to the procedure in most other breeds, but you must always remember that your Poodle has a unique coat. By brushing first you free the hair of mats and tangles. If you did not brush the coat out before bathing these areas, when soaked with water, would become even more matted and tangled and consequently more difficult to brush out without mutilating the coat.

It is necessary to brush your Poodle three or four times a week. This keeps the coat from matting and makes brushing easier each time than it would be if you brushed only once a week. Several brushings a week also makes the brushing-before-the-bath an easier task.

Begin brushing at the hindquarters of the dog. As a matter of fact, all phases should begin here. The dog is less sensitive there than around his face, and by the time you reach the sensitive areas he will have become accustomed to the grooming and won't object.

Brush upward and then downward on the left hind leg, brushing thoroughly and with quick strokes. The brush will alert you to any matting which can be then freed by the use of the comb. Repeat the same process with the right hind leg, then move to the front legs. When the legs are finished begin brushing the body starting at the back end and working toward the front, brushing underneath the body with the same care as on the top. Spend a bit of extra time brushing out your Poodle's topknot, ear hair, and tail pompon, for much of the beauty of your Poodle's appearance emanates from these areas.

Do a good and thorough job and don't try to rush through it in a hurry. If done properly, and if you have trained your Poodle to stand properly when young, brushing can be a pleasurable time for you both. Speak to your Poodle pleasantly during the process of brushing, telling it that this is a fun-time, and you will both approach the brushing or grooming time with anticipatory pleasure in companionship.

Brushing out the tail pompon of a silver Minnie in a "Riviera" Clip.

Brush the hair toward the head and away from the body to allow the soft fullness of the Poodle's coat to show.

14

CHAPTER 4

Bathing and Drying

YOUR POODLE can be bathed once a month, and should be, if you wish to keep it clean and odorless and nice to be near. If your Poodle is white in color it might require more frequent bathing.

Have your shampoo, sponge, brush, towel, tweezers, and other accessories close to the tub and near to hand. Add to the list already mentioned a box of baby cotton-tipped stick cleaners. Attach a hose to the faucet of the tub and lift your Poodle into the tub. Now you are ready to begin.

First put cotton plugs in your dog's ears to keep water out of the ear canals. Use warm but not hot water and soap the dog as you flow the water over its body. Soap and cleanse the body from the neck down first and then clean its head and ears. Be careful not to get soap in the dog's eyes. A shampoo that will not harm or "burn" the dog's eyes is *"Tear-Less."* Mineral oil, a couple of drops in each eye, is also protection.

Remember that a dog's coat naturally rejects water. The body oils and undercoat make it difficult for water to reach the skin, so it is necessary to rub the soap or shampoo into the coat vigorously. Work the lather in thoroughly, then rinse until all sign of soap has vanished. Do not hesitate to repeat the process again if all the accumulated dirt and odor has not been removed. Inci-

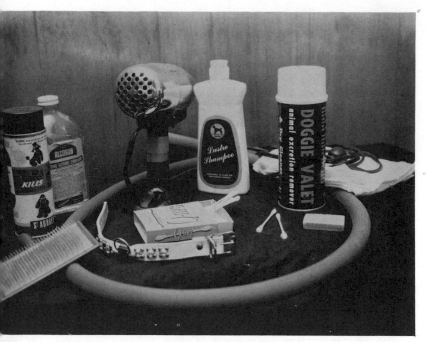

These are the utensils necessary to thoroughly bathe your Poodle. The rubber hose will be attached to the bathtub spigot. The collar should be cleaned with alcohol, and the "Q" tips are for the ears.

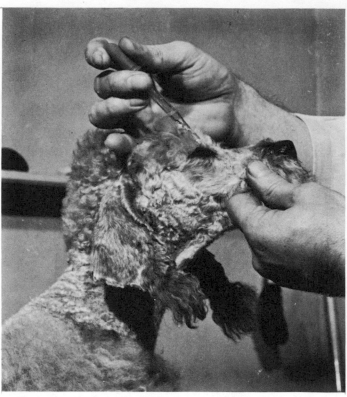

A drop or two of mineral oil in your Poodle's eyes will protect them from soap or shampoo irritants.

dentally, it is a good idea to clean the dog's collar, particularly scrape the inside of it, for it frequently carries the "doggy" odor which we blame on the coat. Cleanse the collar with alcohol. Then rub with a light oil and it will remain clean, odorless and pliable.

While bathing check your Poodle's ears. They can be cleaned with the same type of stick cleaner with a cotton tip that is used to clean a baby's ears. Dip the cotton tip in alcohol and swab it gently around in the ear pocket to remove odorous wax and accumulated dirt. If the odor persists even after constant cleaning, and is accompanied by a crumbly wax, have your Poodle treated by a veterinarian for ear mites or canker.

Rub the shampoo in thoroughly.

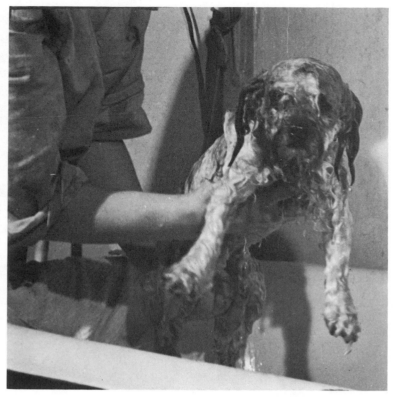
Rinse away all soap or shampoo.

If your Poodle shows any indication of the presence of fleas in his coat it is best to deflea him with a good flea powder the day before you bathe him. There is also a good "dip" to be used in the rinse water, for fleas. The dog owner has a wide variety of soaps to choose from, some designed for special color coats, such as a blue shampoo for silver poodles. Some have defleaing agents present, others don't. The choice is yours as most of them are good.

Remember to protect yourself with a plastic apron for you are going to get wet when your Poodle shakes, a natural reaction of the dog to water. Use the sponge saturated with shampoo to work the cleansing agent deeply into the coat. Remember to clean the feet and the anal region well. A natural bristle brush can also be employed in a circular motion, to get the shampoo down to skin level and remove all dirt. When you are satisfied that your Poodle is thoroughly clean rinse just as completely, leaving no lather anywhere on the body.

To free the body of excess water squeeze gently with a rubbing movement of the hands, then rub briskly with a towel. When you have completed this chore, put the dog in a confined or enclosed area and use the hot air blower to continue the drying process. If you have a drying cage you can complete the drying by simply allowing the dog to remain in the drying cage until it is completely dry.

Fluff Drying

To get that airy, fluffy, powder-puff look one must combine blower drying with brushing. Hot air from the dryer is directed at the area where the brushing is taking place. Incidentally, the hair of your Poodle must not be completely dry, only "damp-

Towel your Poodle dry.

Fluff-drying a Dutch Clip.

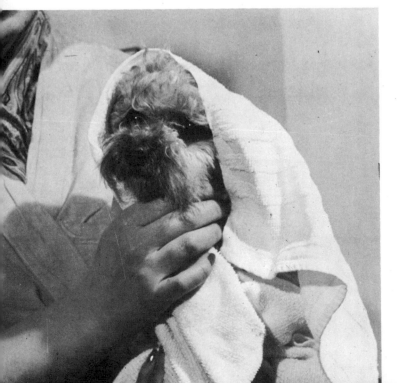
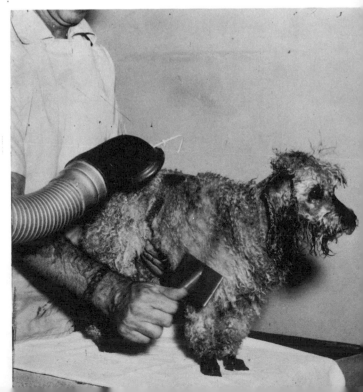

dry", to utilize this special method of "fluff drying." Again, begin with the legs of your Poodle, then do the body and, lastly, the head and ears. Keep the hot air from the dryer directed at the area upon which you are working and, using light and easy strokes, fluff up the Poodle's coat so that each hair is separated and affected by the hot air from the dryer.

When you have fluff dried the dog completely, finish by giving it a quick combing out over the entire body and head.

Remember that bathing and drying are two of the most important steps in arriving at a satisfying finished product, a beautifully groomed and clipped Poodle of gossamer loveliness.

Drying the coat on your Poodle's underparts .

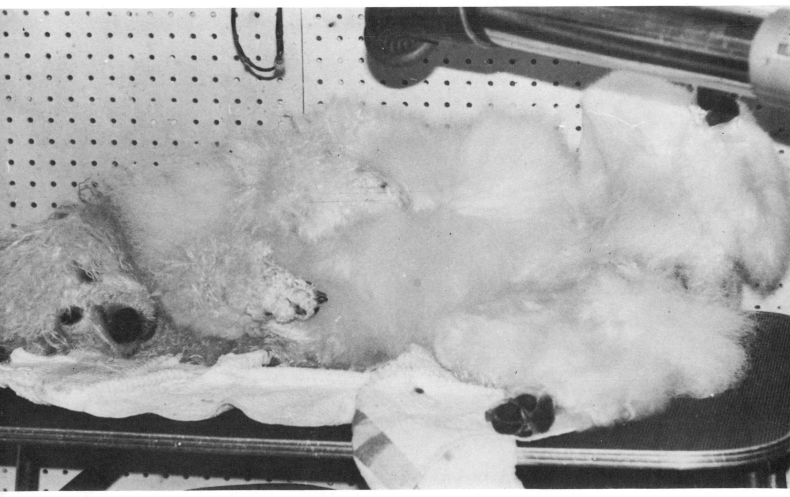

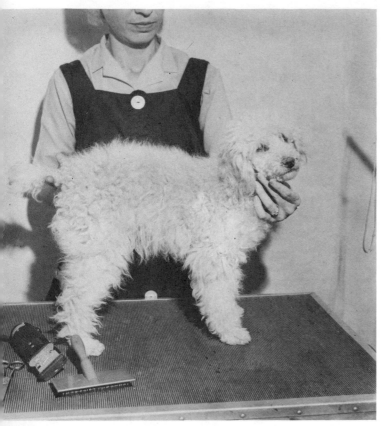

In the rough, before clipping.

Allow the clipper to run so that your Poodle becomes used to the sound, manipulating his feet meanwhile.

Begin by clipping the back feet

Next clip the front feet. Be patient and gentle.

CHAPTER 5
How to Clip Your Poodle

IF YOUR dog has never before been clipped, the sound of the running clipper may disturb him. To keep him from forming a habit-pattern of nervousness and fear that will manifest itself each time you attempt to clip him, the approach this initial time must be made with caution. Put your Poodle on the clipping table and show him the clipper and allow him to sniff it. Then turn the clipper on and hold it in your hand while you talk to him in a light, friendly tone, assuring him that there is nothing to fear from the buzz. Next turn the clipper off and run it through his coat and around his head a few times until he has lost all fear of it. You can then begin the actual operation of clipping him quietly and gently talking as you cut to calm his natural fears.

Hold the flat of the clipper blade against the surface you are clipping. If you tip it forward it will dig in and cause unsightly cut marks. Remember not to cut against the grain or lay of the hair, always clip with the grain. Later, when you have become expert, there may be some areas (around the lips, throat, etc.) where you will perhaps want to cut closer and, with the skill you have acquired, it will be possible for you to clip against the lay of the hair. Actually, only a show Poodle need ever be trimmed this closely. The ordinary house pet doesn't need as fine a finish as the show Poodle. Cutting against the grain can cause sharp and uneven crevices in the clipped area and burn the dog's tender skin causing scabs to form. The burning of clipper cutting against the grain can build an avid dislike for the whole business in the mind of your Poodle, and he will forever after be difficult to manage during the clipping process. Start clipping your Poodle when he is young, anytime after three months of age. Begin by clipping the feet, base of tail and foreface. If he raises an objection when you know you are not hurting him, be firm, insist that he stand for his barbering and, after a time or two, he will become accustomed to the process and will either be eager for the attention clipping brings or bored with the whole thing.

The first time you clip your Poodle be content with simply using the clippers, particularly if it is also the first time for your dog. Once both you and the dog gain confidence you can graduate to the use of the other tools. When using the shears always have the points angled away from the dog's eyes for a quick move by the dog can be disastrous.

Your Poodle's face and head are the most difficult parts of the animal to clip. He can move his head much faster than his body and it is a much smaller area in which to work. The head can be

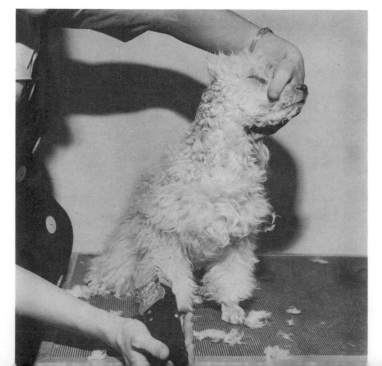

Allow the clippers to again run a few minutes before starting on your Poodle's face.

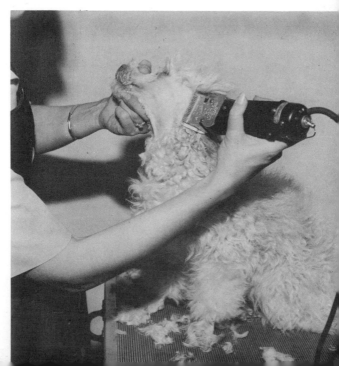

Curl your fingers around his muzzle to hold your Poodle steady and to protect the mustache if one is to be left.

controlled best when one hand of the operator holds the dog's muzzle and the other hand works the clippers. Usually, when the muzzle is to be clipped clean, the hand holding it is above the foreface with thumb and fingers curling down over the muzzle. But in clips where a mustache is to be left, such as the Royal Dutch clip, the hand should be held under the jaw with the fingers curled up around the muzzle to protect the mustache.

The Poodle's lips are particularly difficult to clip close and clean without nipping. When clipping the hair from the edge of the lip. carefully pull back the corner of the mouth with the fingers holding the muzzle to cause the lip-edge hair to bristle away from the skin. When clipping the under neck for a Dutch trim, hold the dog's head up, muzzle pointing toward the ceiling. Always keep in mind the lines of demarcation you have visualized for the clip you are endeavoring to accomplish, for once hair is cut it cannot be pasted back and you will have to wait until it has grown in again.

The Poodle's feet are a bit touchy to clip and you will find that he will attempt to pull them back when you work on them. This is one place where you will often have to cut against the

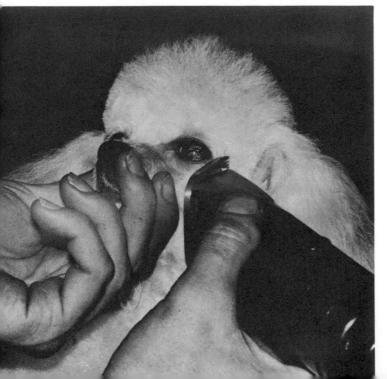

Clip with the grain, or lay, of the hair.

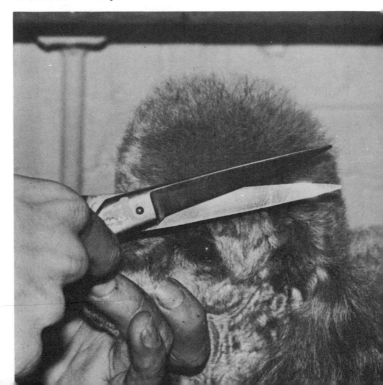

The topknot or head pompon must be scissored evenly.

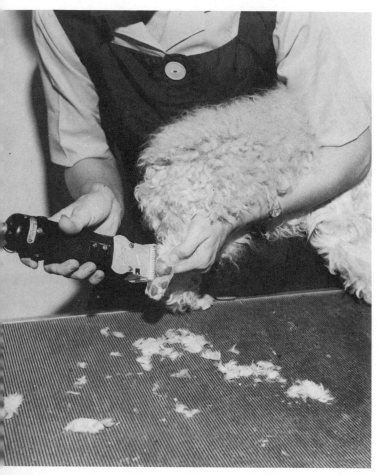

Clip the hair between the pads of the feet.

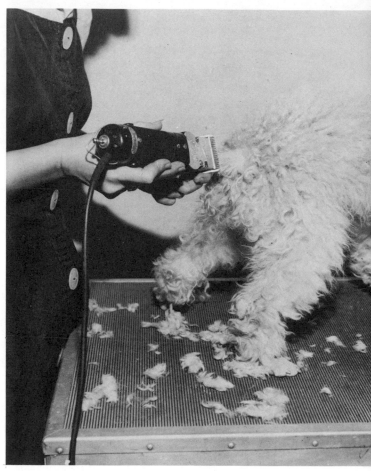

The tail should be clipped halfway down to the body.

grain of the hair. Remember to cut the hair that grows from between the pads at the bottom of the feet. When cutting the hair between the toes be careful not to nick the web that stretches between the toes. To trim the back feet get behind the dog so that his back is toward you. You will find this an easier way to work in that area.

The tail should be clipped halfway down and clean to where it meets the body. The tassel left at the tip should be fluffed out and then trimmed with the shears to form a ball.

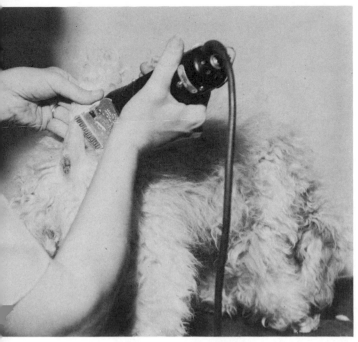 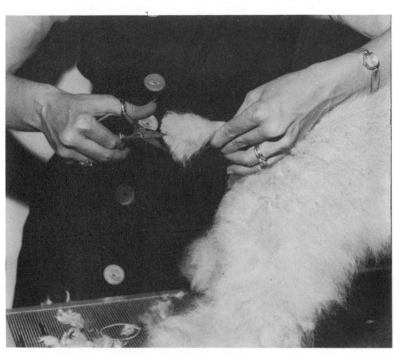

Clipping the underside of the tail. Use straight scissors to get the tail pompon. even

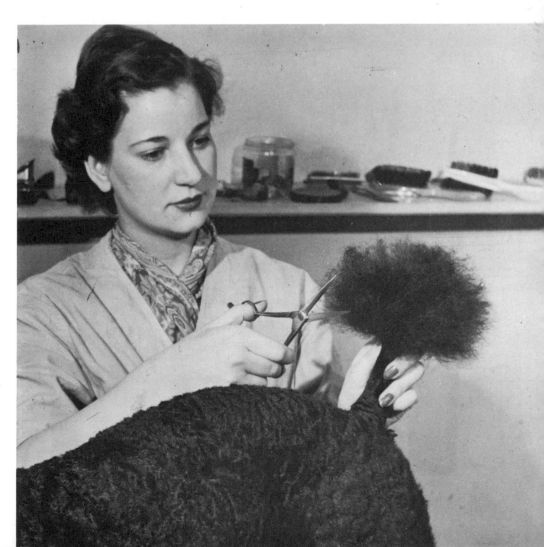

Comb out the tail
pompon and scissor away
any unevenness in the outline.

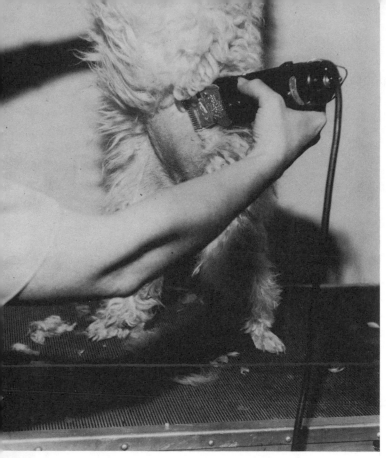

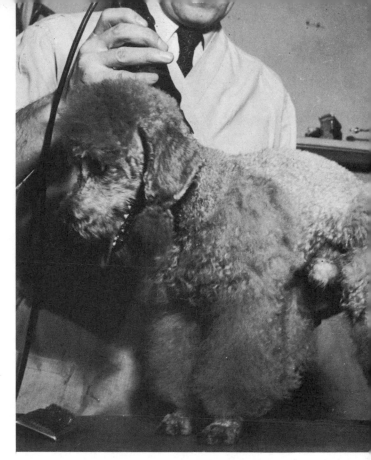

Clipping the underbelly of a Miniature (or Toy).

Clipping the back in the Dutch Clip.

To clip the underbelly, the dog, if a toy or miniature, should be rolled over on its back or, standing behind it as when the back feet are clipped, grasp the hind legs and lift them up so that the Poodle is standing on his front legs only, then run the clippers along the belly line.

The back is the easiest part of the Poodle to clip. When executing the Dutch clip place the flat of the blade facing toward the dog's rear and begin directly behind the head pompadour running the clipper the full length of the back from the back of the skull to the tail set.

The hip and leg pompons that identify the Continental clip can be marked on the coat with colored chalk with the first clipping so that they will be placed even on both sides of the dog.

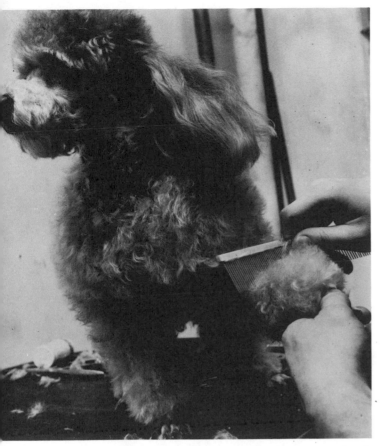

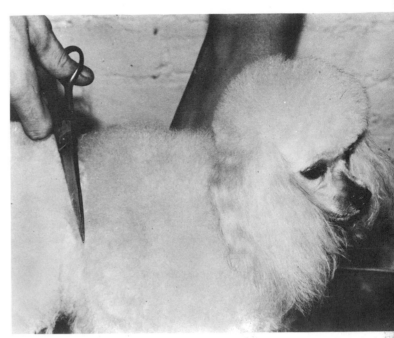

Stray ends that spoil the outline and dull the crispness of the pattern can be scissored away to produce a smooth and finished end result.

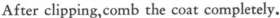

After clipping, comb the coat completely.

When you have completed the job of clipping, comb the hair out and view the result from different angles to get the full effect of your handiwork. You will see stray ends that spoil the outline and can go to work with the shears to even up and smooth the finished product.

You will probably be exhausted after the first attempt at clipping, but, when you see what you have accomplished, you will agree that the results have justified the effort. And you can bask in the knowledge that each time you clip your Poodle the task will be easier as you gain skill and sureness. Aside from this satisfaction, think of the money you saved!

CHAPTER 6
The Basic Clip

THE BASIC CLIP is the first clip you will give your Poodle. You can BASIC CLIP a six weeks old puppy and keep it in this clip until it is about four months old. From then, until the Poodle has reached maturity, or is 12 months old, the PUPPY CLIP is used. Upon maturity, or after the dog has reached the age of 12 months, one of the adult clips of your choice can fashion the lines of its silhouette.

THE BASIC CLIP includes brushing, bathing, fluff drying, and the clipping of the face, feet and tail. This BASIC CLIP is the most important clip of all, for from it you will learn how to manipulate the tools of grooming, how to handle your dog during the process of clipping, and all other fundamentals, for all other clips are but elaborations of this, the BASIC CLIP.

Use a No. 15 blade. This is an all round utility blade and should be used for the BASIC CLIP entirely. In the BASIC CLIP we begin with the face, then do the feet, and lastly the tail.

Face

To begin, hold the dog's muzzle in your hand with the ear pulled around the back of the head and held by the same hand. This leaves the side of the head free for the clippers. Now, place the blade of the clipper at the ear and clip in one long, easy stroke,

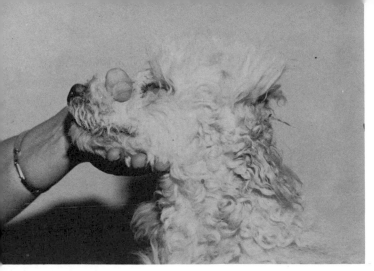

Beginning the Basic Clip.

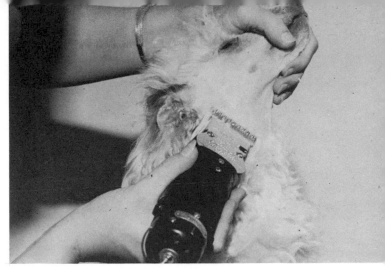

First clip the face, using a No. 15 blade.

to the corner of the eye. Now, go back to your starting point at the ear and, with a similar stroke, move the clipper head slightly lower and toward the corner of the mouth. The mouth must next engage your attention. Hold the lips taut and slightly stretched for this operation and clip carefully around the mouth. Repeat what you have done on the other side of the face. Then run the clippers on the underjaw to where the head and neck connect (the throat latch). Neck clipping should not be done now as it is included in the body clip. To complete the face clip–

After the face is finished, clip the feet.

Clipping the sensitive area between the toes.

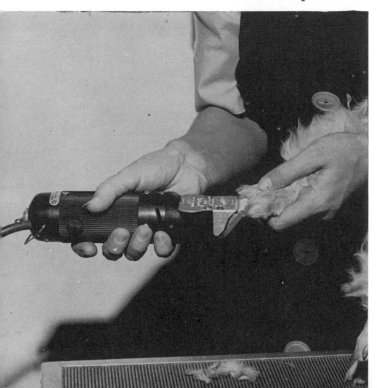

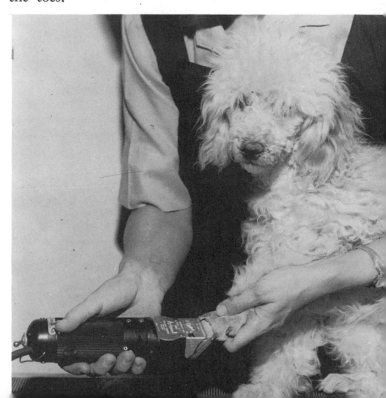

ping bring the clipper blade level with the eyes and clip down the muzzle to the nose. Never clip toward the eyes and never clip *above* the eyes.

Feet

Clipping the paws is difficult because of the animal's sensitivity in this area. Work slowly and carefully for the paw has many and close angles. Clip the hair clean up to the ankles. Clean the back of the paw and then get ready for the most difficult task of all, the clipping of the hair between the toes. Hold the paw in your hand and spread the toes. You will see that the feet are webbed, the webbing being between the toes. You must be

Clever clipping can correct the tail that has been incorrectly docked, and make it appear perfect •

Spray to produce gloss, body, and to condition the coat •

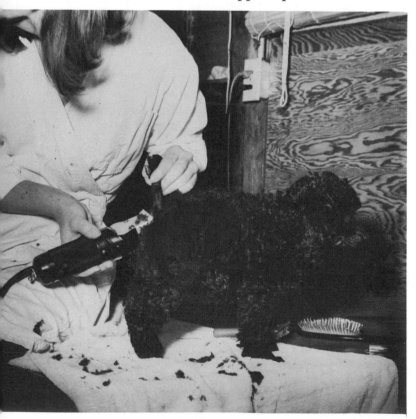

careful not to cut the web with your clippers. Use a rocking, or side-to-side motion, and handle the clippers lightly in this sensitive area.

Tail

Arrange to leave a full pompon on the tail, regardless of its length. Often Poodle tails are cropped incorrectly, but clever clipping can make them appear perfect. Clip bare a section of about one and a half inches to the base of the tail muff (this for Miniatures).

CHAPTER 7
The Puppy Clip

THE PET Poodle's coat will not take on the heaviness and body of maturity until after the dog is a year old. Up to that time the easily accomplished PUPPY CLIP can be used. Use the No. 15 blade and handle your clippers, etc. exactly as you did in the BASIC CLIP.

In the PUPPY CLIP the face, feet and the bottom half of the tail are clipped clean. The tail pompon is shaped round with the shears and the hair on the head, ears, neck, body and legs is combed out and trimmed slightly with the shears to present a pleasing silhouette.

Beginning the Puppy Clip.

Clipping the muzzle.

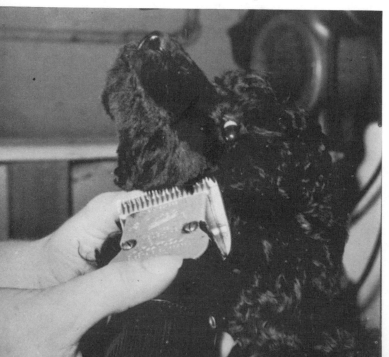

The Puppy Clip in
the show ring worn by
a young Standard Poodle.
A Poodle can be shown in this
clip until it is a year old.

Diagramatic drawing
of the Puppy Clip. Note
the gentle slope from skull to tail.

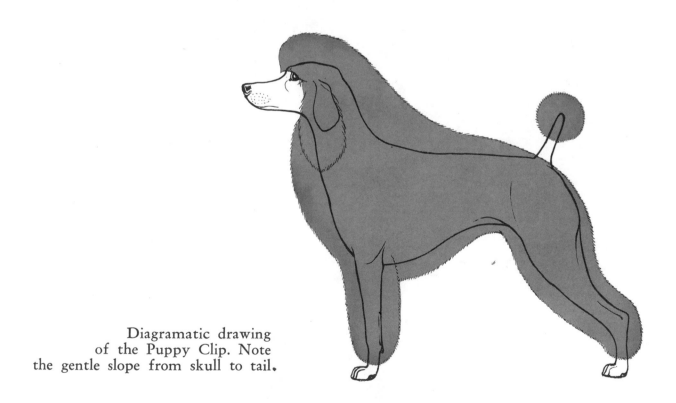

CHAPTER 8
The Show Clips

WHEN THE Poodle reaches show ring maturity you clip to the variations of the English Saddle clip. The face, base of tail, feet, legs and the sections of body as shown in the illustration, are clipped clean and close. One pompon is left on the front legs and two on the hind legs. The blanket on the hindquarters is trimmed medium close to exhibit the close and heavy Persian lamb curl. The hair of the topknot, mane and ears is left long. The leg and tail pompons are also left long but slightly trimmed to shape.

Clipping front legs in English Saddle Clip. One Pompon is left on front legs, two on rear legs.

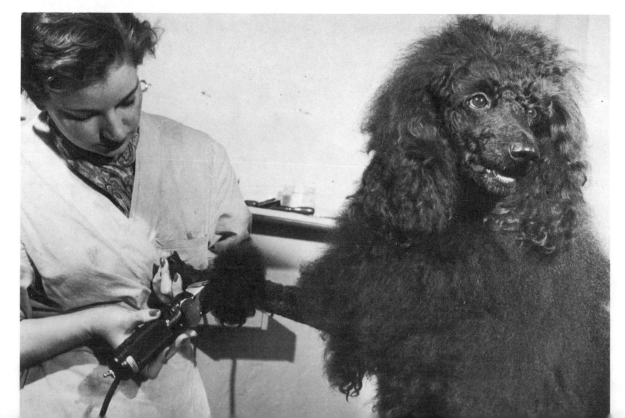

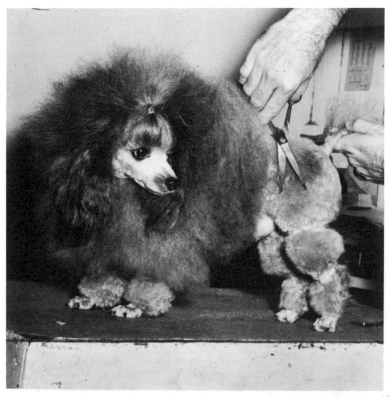

Trimming the blanket in the English Saddle Clip.

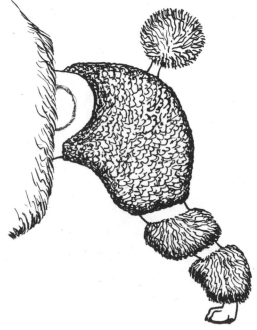

Rear section showing English Saddle Clip. The blanket, or "Pack" runs into the rear part of the mane, and a "kidney patch" is cut out. This patch has been shrinking in size over the years.

Diagrammatic drawing of the English Saddle Clip

The English Saddle Clip is the ultimate test of a Poodle groomer's skill. The expert can lay the pattern of an English Saddle Clip so that the dog looks absolutely perfect in every detail.

The Continental clip is basically the same as the English Saddle and it is easy to convert to this clip from either the Puppy or English Saddle clip. The obvious difference between the English Saddle and the Continental is the lack of the curly saddle in the latter clip. Also the upper bracelet on the hind legs is deleted and a rosette added to the hip.

An important feature of all three of the show clips is the fullness of the mane. It must be combed to stand out, away from the body, to form the fluffy halo of hair around the dog that is the trademark of the breed.

Clipping the hindquarters in the Continental Clip.

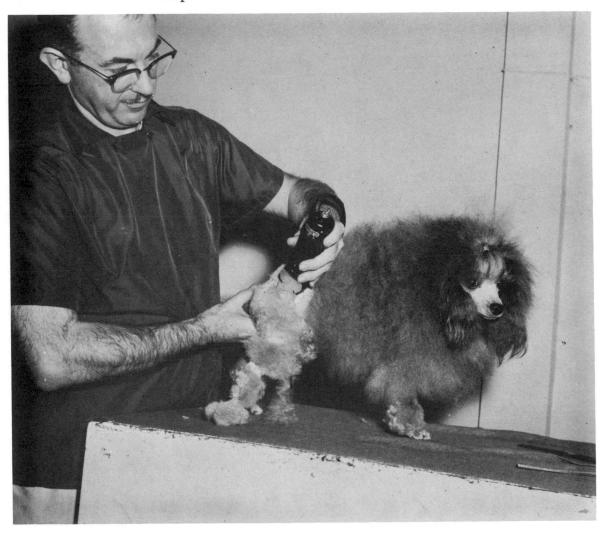

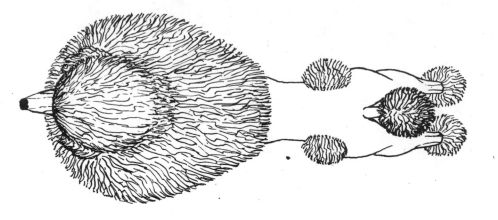

Bird's eye view of Continental Clip

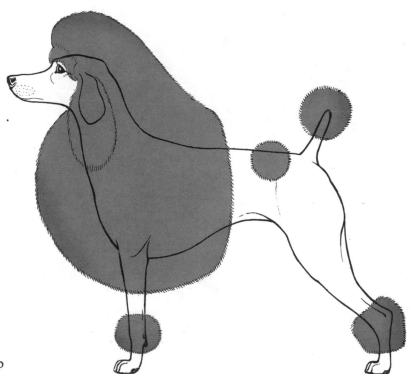

Diagrammatic view of Continental Clip

A Poodle sporting a Continental Clip in the show ring. This clip is becoming increasingly popular for show dogs, particularly Poodles of the Standard variety such as the dog in our illustration.

Incidentally, for show ring purposes, the Poodle is divided into three distinct size brackets: the Standard Poodle, the Miniature Poodle, and the Toy Poodle. The Standard is the largest and must be fifteen inches or over at the shoulder. Many Standards mature into very large and impressive animals. The Miniature must be under fifteen inches at the shoulder but over ten inches; and the Toy Poodle under ten inches. Some Toys, called "sleeve" dogs (from the ancient Chinese when Mandarins carried favorite, tiny toy dogs in their sleeves) are very small, often weighing no more than three or four pounds. The size limits of the Miniature, being in the middle as it were, are obviously more rigid.

Toy Poodles are shown in the ring under the Toy category. Miniature and Standard Poodles are shown in the non-sporting classes. Actually the large Standard Poodle should be listed as a Sporting Dog for they are fine water dogs and make excellent retrievers.

It should be mentioned here that many years ago there was another approved coat type in Poodles, the Corded Poodle. The coat was allowed to grow without clipping or brushing and was oiled to prevent hair from breaking. Treated in such a manner the coat formed thin, round mats of hair which, when allowed to become long, formed a mass of ropelike cords to the floor. It was a coat fad and certainly not a very sanitary one. The odorous, matted hair that made the Corded Poodle would not be tolerated in our more enlightened age.

The three size varieties of Poodles. On the left, a Toy Poodle in a Lamb Clip. In the middle a Miniature Poodle, and the large black Poodle in the English Saddle Clip is a Standard.

CHAPTER 9
The Dutch Clip

OF ALL clips the DUTCH is probably the most difficult to execute correctly. Of course the SHOW CLIPS are difficult because, if the dog is to be shown, these clips must be perfect.

Never forget the basic grooming procedure no matter what clip is used. By that I mean the brushing, bathing, fluff drying and BASIC CLIPPING before proceeding with any new clip. Of course, if the ROYAL DUTCH CLIP with a MUSTACHE is to be done, cleaning of the muzzle as in the BASIC CLIP must be modified.

Use your No. 15 blade for the neck and, clipping with the grain, move the clippers from the base of the skull down the

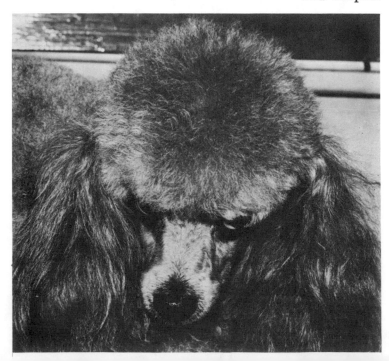

Muzzle clipped smooth in modified Dutch Clip. The ears have yet to be clipped and the ear-end tassels left and shaped.

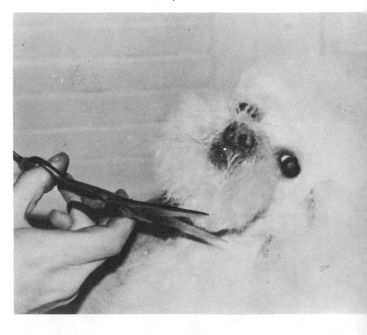

If the mustache is left, scissor it even.

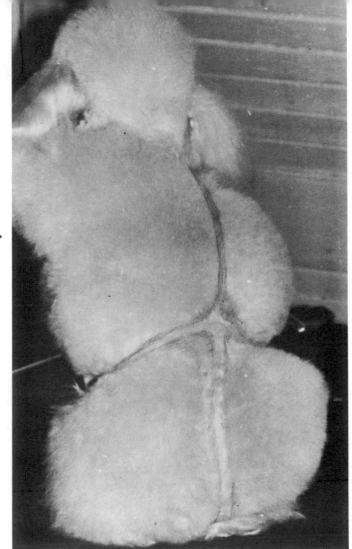

Body stripes
or cross bands
in the Dutch Clip.

middle of the back to the base of the tail. This last bit of clipping can be accomplished with the 5/8 Poodle or Dutch blade, made particularly for this clip. Make the dog sit squarely so the line will be straight. After you become proficient you can, using this same blade, begin at the base of the tail and move the clippers upward toward the neck against the grain to make the DUTCH stripe.

Use the same 5/8 blade for the cross band that goes around the body, starting it from the middle band on the neck. This 5/8 blade width is perfect for Minnies and Toys. Larger Poodles will require a No. 15 blade width. Incidentally, this DUTCH CLIP looks best on Miniatures and Toys.

In the ROYAL DUTCH CLIP the feet, neck, middle body band, all of the ear except the tassel, all of the face except the mustache, the bottom half of the tail and a string along the middle of the back, are clipped close and clean. The facial "whiskers" are left unclipped and combed forward, the head pompon is trimmed to a graduated "V" on the neck. Ear tassels are left on the clean ear and are combed down. The rest of the body, which is unclipped, is trimmed with shears to remove any raggedness from the outline.

In the three SHOW CLIPS there can be no innovation if the animal is to be shown, and the Kennel clip serves its purpose admirably as it is. But, in the DUTCH CLIP, modifications can be indulged in. Many owners clean the muzzle completely, clipping off the mustache or whiskers but allowing the DUTCH CLIP otherwise to remain as it is. Poodle owners who have a pet house dog claim that it is easier to keep the animal clean with a clipped muzzle since it keeps food particles from catching in the whiskers and water from soaking this extra hair growth when the Poodle drinks.

The Royal Dutch
Clip, a diagrammatic
sketch for full understanding

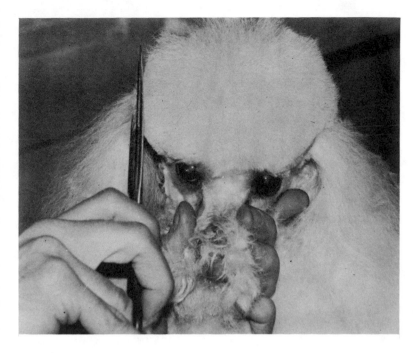

Trimming the topknot, or head pompon, in the Dutch Clip. This is a modified Dutch, leaving the ear hair full.

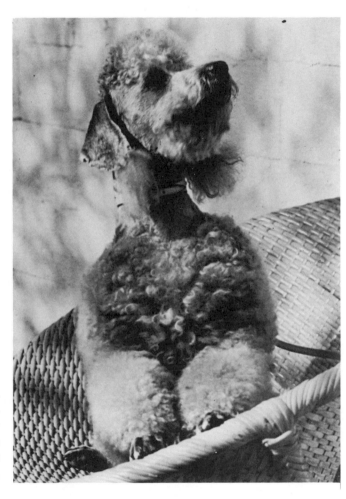

The Royal Dutch Clip completed in full detail. This Miniature certainly looks both comfortable and regal in his Royal Dutch Clip.

Other modifications that can be wrought in the basic DUTCH CLIP is to eliminate the neck "V" and shape the head pompon round, and shape the hindquarters cut to resemble the back end of the English Saddle clip.

The DUTCH CLIP lends itself readily to improvisation by the imaginative owner and this is a good thing. It's your dog and your clippers, so have fun.

CHAPTER 10
The Lamb Clip

FOR THE pet Poodle the LAMB CLIP is beginning to rival the DUTCH CLIP in popularity. As a matter of fact it is an easier clip than the DUTCH and is more easily maintained.

We begin with the BASIC CLIP, using the No. 15 blade for feet, face and tail. Now we change to a blue blade which is the main blade we will use for the LAMB CLIP. Beginning at the base of the skull, as we did in the DUTCH CLIP, run the blade in a straight line, with the grain or lay of the hair, down to the base of the tail, using the spine as a guide rule.

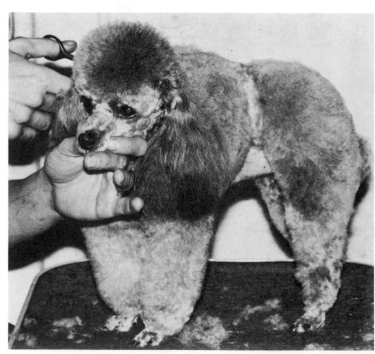

Trimming back of head pompon with scissors in Lamb Clip.

Next clip a smooth line that comes from the middle line and outlines the legs, front and rear. The legs are going to be left in a full pantaloon. Keeping the blade flat (as you must always do no matter what portion of the body is being clipped), run it around the body, cleaning off the torso and not forgetting the under-body. To accomplish the latter, hold the dog up by his two front feet so that he is standing.

Next clean off the neck with the No. 5 blade so that it matches the body. Incidentally, the No. 5 blade will clip no closer to the body than 1/2 inch. Now comb out the hair on the legs and chest so that it stands away from the skin.

Next, with the No. 5 blade again, delicately blend the edges of the full-coated legs with the clipped body. This blending technique takes a light stroke that will take a bit of time to learn.

Combing out the Lamb Clip

Scissor off all stray hair.

Scissor the topknot to a clean, smooth pompon.

Using The Scissors

Before using the scissors, spray the entire animal with a good coat dressing. Brush and comb the dressing spray into the coat until it is dry and then you can begin scissoring. First scissor the region around the ankle joint, then work up the leg, trimming away any stray hair that destroys the smoothness of the outline.

Now we come to the tail. Carefully twist the hair of the tail in your fingers and, holding it out, cut the edge of the hair close to your fingers and straight across. Shake out and you will have a pompon. Now is the time to use your curved scissors to edge the tail pom and make it round and even. With the straight scissors, trim away any hair that destroys the outline with particular attention given to the rectal area.

The last place to scissor is the topknot. Here again use the curved scissors to get a smooth outline and roundness all around.

Now stand away from the dog for a few moments and examine it. Perhaps it needs a touch here or there. You will learn with experience how to add those little finishing touches that make for beauty.

Diagram of Lamb Clip

E·A·HART

CHAPTER 11
The Town and Country Clip

THIS TIME you will use a No. 10 blade to accomplish the TOWN AND COUNTRY CLIP. As a matter of fact this clip is much like the LAMB CLIP. The coat on the shoulder area is left rather high and clearly set off from the body, for there is no blending of the body and the edges of the longer coat on the front legs.

Instead of the 1/2 inch length of coat left by the No. 5 blade, we use the No. 10 blade instead so that we can cut closer and leave a 1/4 inch length of coat where the clippers are used.

This clip is for the dog that lives in rural areas and is similar to some of the sporting clips occasionally seen worn by Poodles that are being used as gun or sporting water dogs.

Diagram of Town and Country Clip.

Combing out the Town and Country Clip.

Trim off all ragged hairs with scissors.

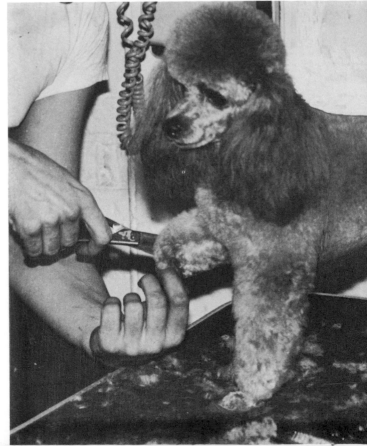

CHAPTER 12
The Summer Clip

THIS CLIP is designed to keep the Poodle comfortable during the hot "dog" days of full summer. For the SUMMER CLIP use a No. 10 blade on the entire body and legs with the exception of the bracelets on the legs which are left full and scissored into round pompons. Allow the ears, topknot and tail pompon to remain full also, scissoring slightly to evenness. The latter job to be done with the curved scissors.

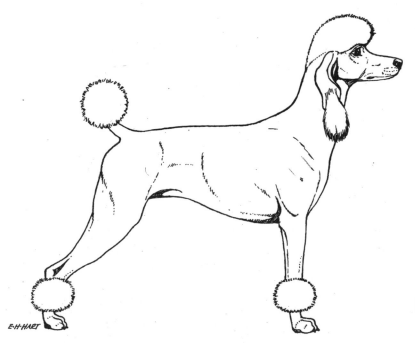

Drawing of Summer Clip

CHAPTER 13
The Kennel Clip

THE KENNEL CLIP is easily accomplished and easy to maintain. When several or many dogs are kept in a kennel they can, in a KENNEL CLIP, always be neat and clean appearing. Another virtue inherent in this clip is its closeness to the basic show clips. By allowing the coat to achieve a bit more fullness the KENNEL CLIP can readily be fashioned to a Puppy, English Saddle or Continental clip.

In the KENNEL CLIP the face, feet and lower half of the tail are clipped clean. The hair on the head pompon, ears and tail pompon is left long but shaped to a pleasing outline with the shears. The neck and body is clipped to approximately one inch length (longer on larger Standard Poodles), to exhibit the tight, Persian lamb curl for which the breed is noted. The hair on the legs is scissored to approximately double the length of the body hair.

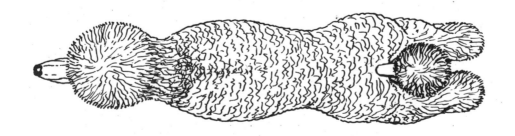

The Kennel Clip

Clipping the
muzzle in the
Kennel Clip. It
must be clipped clean.

Scissor the
head pompon to
slick roundness, clip-
ping off all stray hair
that destroys the outline.

CHAPTER 14
Mustaches and Color Tinting

THERE ARE several types of MUSTACHES (or moustaches, if you prefer). Among the favorites are the German, the Van Buren, the Donut, the French, and the Sweetheart mustache.

There are many Poodle owners who do not like to have mustaches on their pets because food can accumulate on mustache hairs and become another area that needs constant care and extra grooming.

But, if you think that your dog looks cute with a mustache, and many do, particularly if in a ROYAL DUTCH CLIP, then you must cover the area at the end of the dog's muzzle where the mustache grows with your hand when you clip. The Mustache itself must be trimmed to evenness with the shears.

The GERMAN MUSTACHE is shaven on the top of the nose but not on the lower jaw. The FRENCH MUSTACHE

The German Mustache

The French Mustache

The Sweetheart Mustache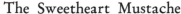The Van Buren Mustache

has the top of the nose and the lower jaw cleaned close. The DONUT MUSTACHE has neither top nor bottom shaven and is scissored into a round shape. The VAN BUREN has a deep beardlike effect that merges with what we might call "sideburns." The top of the nose is sometimes clipped close. The SWEETHEART MUSTACHE is clipped close toward the nose to appear heartshaped, then scissored short.

Color Tinting

Of course color tinting only works well with white or light colored dogs. The vehicle should be a good vegetable dye that is harmless to babies and animals and will wash off easily. Simply fill a large receptacle or tub with warm water and stir in the desired color until the tint has been achieved that most touches your aesthetic sense. Now give your Poodle its regular bath. Then, while the dog is still in the tub and wet, pour the tinted water over him with a separate pan, working it into the coat as you would a rinse. Then towel the dog and continue with the rest of the grooming procedure as usual.

CHAPTER 15
The Professional Dog Groomer

THERE ARE schools for individuals who wish to become professional dog groomers, where courses can be had for this specific purpose. But it is not necessary to take such a course to become a professional dog groomer if you have served a long apprenticeship and are positive that you know your business thoroughly. Neither is such a course or schooling required by law in order to engage in professional dog grooming as a full time vocation.

It is, in fact, a very nice way to earn a living and you can combine hobby and work in one pleasurable and financially satisfactory business. The investment necessary to begin such a busi-

Scraping tartar from teeth is a chore the professional knows how to handle.

Trimming around the lips must be done with skill.

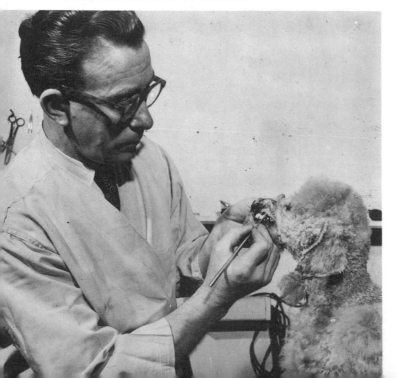

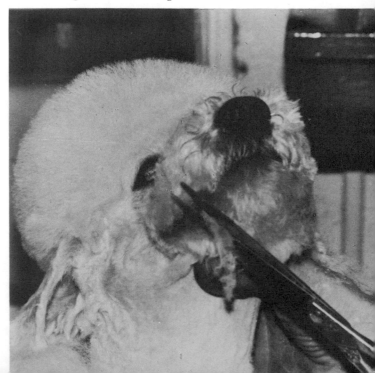

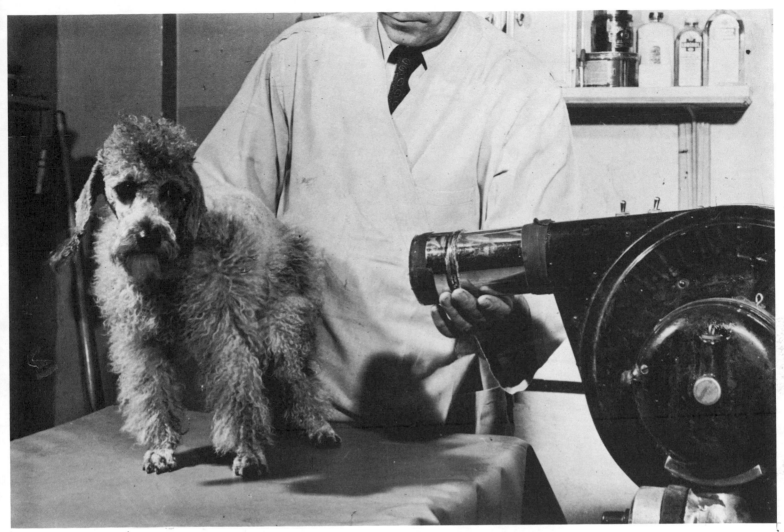

The proper equipment is a "must" for the professional.

ness is comparatively very small. As a matter of fact, anyone who contemplates entering into the grooming field professionally will have had a good deal of experience behind them, during which time they have probably accumulated much of the equipment necessary to launch them in the business professionally.

We will assume that you have the basic tools, therefore, such as; clippers, blades, scissors, shampoos, etc. Your main investment then will be in cages and a good tub.

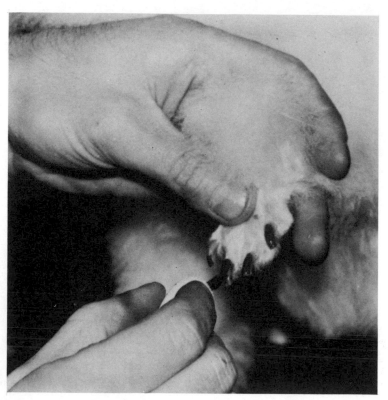

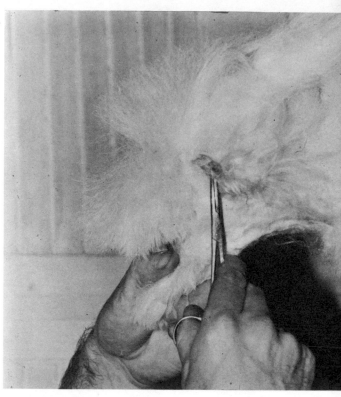

Finishing touch for the nails.

Removing excess hair from the ears.

It is best to invest a little more initially in your cages and get the best new metal cages, preferably aluminum. A drying cage is also a necessity. Or one can be made from an ordinary cage with heating coils, electric bulbs, or the special heating units made especially for dogs, and a little ingenuity on your part.

The tub must be raised from the ground to make bathing easier for you, and you will need a floor dryer for "fluffing" Another "must" is a good vacuum cleaner to keep clipped hair from accumulating.

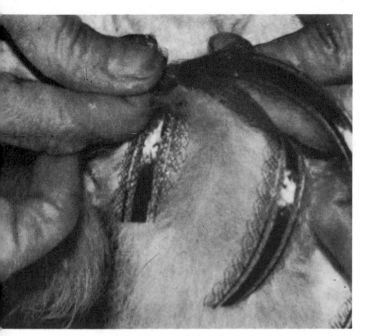

An added bit of finish . . . a bow
for my Poodle's ear.

"Papillotte" wrappings, of cotton
and plastic, applied by Poodle
beautician.

Always keep your place neat and clean and find a good location to set up shop. This selection of the locale for your salon is important as is the selection of location for any business. Do not open up in a place where there are too many dog grooming salons and competition is too great. A newcomer will find it hard to survive in an area of long established salons. But there are many areas where there is little or no competition and lots of opportunity for a good dog grooming salon.

Do a good and competent job in which you, as a professional, can take pride. Charge a decent but not exhorbitant fee, and keep your salon clean and attractive looking and you will never want for clients.

CHAPTER 16
Mimic and Fun Clips

YOUR POODLE lends itself to many clip disguises. He can appear to be any one of a number of other breeds. Certainly if the German Shepherd can be erroneously called a "Police Dog," then the Poodle can very well be named a "Detective Dog," for with clever handling of clippers and shears he can be made to appear to be a breed he isn't.

Of course Poodles of all sizes can be trimmed to the various disguises, but if they are to appear authentic they must stay within the size and color range of the breed they are to mimic. As an example, a white Toy Poodle could easily be given a KERRY BLUE TERRIER CLIP but would not be very convincing as

The Kerry Blue Clip.

Cleaning the neck in
the Kerry Blue Clip.

a Kerry since the Kerry's coat color is black to dark blue (at maturity) and he stands from 18 to 19 inches at the shoulder. You can readily see that, to mimic the Kerry Blue, a large Miniature or small Standard Poodle must be used and, to make the disguise complete, he should be either a black or a blue.

The KERRY CLIP is well adapted to a Poodle disguise. The coat of the Kerry, unlike most terriers, is soft, dense and wavy. To give your Poodle the Kerry clip, clean the ears, skull, cheeks and neck closely. Allow eyebrows and all hair on the top, sides and bottom of the muzzle to remain and comb it forward toward the nose. Clip the tail completely and fairly close. Clip shoulders and body moderately, leaving the hair about an inch long so that it will curl and form a close, tight mat over the entire body. The hair on the chest can be cut slightly closer than that on the body. Allow about two inches of hair to remain on the legs and comb it down so that it covers the feet. The finish, to complete the disguise outline, can be done with shears and razor-blade plucking dresser.

The SCHNAUZER type lends itself admirably to a disguise clip. And, since this breed comes in three sizes, Miniature, Standard and Giant, all three Poodle sizes can be used. The Giant Schnauzer is not in the Terrier Group but is considered a Working Dog. But, the clip remains the same as that used on the smaller Schnauzers. A large black Standard Poodle can readily mimic a Giant Schnauzer in a disguise clip.

Grey Poodles most closely approach the salt-and-pepper color associated with the Schnauzer. The most ideal color would be a Phantom Poodle, or one whose coat varies from a darker grey on the body to lighter grey on the face, chest, underbody and legs. But, since the A.K.C. Poodle standard calls for only solid colors in the breed, there aren't too many Phantoms to be found.

The Schnauzer Clip

Schnauzers have their ears cropped and their tails cut close, but in England the ears are left natural so, in the disguise clip, your Poodle will look more like an English Schnauzer than an American representative of the breed. In the process of clipping him you can give him a clipped accent, too, and so further the English concept.

Clip the body hair rather close for the SCHNAUZER CLIP. Clean the neck, skull and the top line of the nose. Leave the eyebrows and whiskers long and comb them forward. When clipping the body underline, allow the longer hair to remain on the bottom of the chest behind the front legs and graduate the cut to close as it slopes to the belly. Leg hair should be left long and combed out and cut with shears to the desired outline.

The BEDLINGTON CLIP should be the property of a white Miniature, or a very pale grey Miniature. To be completely effective the skull must not be clipped clean, the hair must be rounded and tapered gradually toward the nose. The muzzle and jaw are clipped clean and a tassel is left on the close clipped ear,

The Bedlington Terrier Clip

much the same as the ear tassel in the Dutch clip. The back is the important part of the Bedlington clip. Clip the coat closely on the neck and withers, then graduate the clip as you move toward the hindquarters, leaving more hair growth in the middle of the back to arrive at the typical roached-back appearance of the Bedlington Terrier. Begin to shear closer again as you reach the set-on of the tail. If properly executed, the back should present a rounded appearance, higher in the middle than at either end. The rest of the body should be clipped medium close. The under-line of the body should be left with more coat on the bottom rib section, close to the front legs, than on the rear belly part, which should be cropped closely. In clipping the legs allow slightly less hair to remain than in the other terrier clips previously described. The tail presents a problem since the Bedlington has a full-length tail and the Poodle doesn't. In this case we must do what we can with what we have. Taper the tail in the clip by allowing slightly more hair to remain at the base than at the closely cropped tip.

Sealyham Clip

This is the type of long, low-stationed Poodle that will look good in a Sealyham Clip.

In Poodles we occasionally find a low-stationed dog, or one that is short in the legs and long in the body. If it happens to be white and a large Miniature, it will lend itself admirably to a SEALYHAM TERRIER disguise.

To accomplish this clip the skull and ears are to be sheared close. Eyebrows and whiskers must be allowed to remain; comb them forward and shape them with your shears. The neck, and a section of the underjaw where it meets the neck, is clipped close as are the shoulders. Graduate your clip down the sides of the dog and allow the hair underneath to remain long combing it down to bring the body as close to the ground as possible. Leave medium hair on the chest and legs and shape with shears. The tail should have enough hair left on to appear short and stumpy.

To lend authenticity to a WIRE-HAIRED FOX TERRIER CLIP we should select a white Miniature. Clip the ears clean; the skull the same. Allow the eyebrows to remain and enough hair along the nose line to give the head an appearance of one long line. Clean the cheeks and under the neck where the jaw joins the neck, but allow the muzzle whiskers to remain. Eyebrows and whiskers can be trimmed to shape with the shears after they are combed forward. The neck should be clipped clean, graduating the cut as it joins the back and shoulders. Clip the front clean but allow enough hair to remain on the back to create a faint curl. The tail should be rather thick and even throughout

The Wire-haired and Irish Terrier Clip

its length. The hair on the legs should be full and even with the ends of the toes. This can be best accomplished by judicious use of the shears. Slightly more hair must be left on the front portion of the underline than on the rear or belly line.

The same clip as described above can be used to turn your Poodle into an IRISH TERRIER. Again a Miniature is most appropriate. But the color is important in this case. Any of the reddish colors can be selected and a deep Apricot is about as close to the color of the Irish coat as can be found in the Poodle.

More Mimic Clips

There are three Sporting Dog clips to which the coat of the Poodle lends itself admirably: the CURLY-COATED RE-TRIEVER, THE AMERICAN WATER SPANIEL and the IRISH WATER SPANIEL CLIPS. Unfortunately (or perhaps

The Curly-coated Retriever Clip

fortunately for them) these three breeds have full length tails, not docked as is the Poodle's. Therefore, when using these clips, we will have to assume that the individual in question has mislaid a portion of his stern. Incidentally, it is considered quite possible that the Poodle descended from the same basic type of animal as did the Water Spaniel and the Curly-coated Retriever. The similarity in coat quality would seem to bear this theory out.

Both the CURLY-COATED RETRIEVER and the IRISH WATER SPANIEL masquerade clips require a Standard Poodle's size to make them believable. For the American Water Spaniel, a large Miniature or small to medium Standard Poodle can be used. The color standard for these Sporting breeds calls for solid liver for all three, but the AMERICAN WATER SPANIEL and the CURLY-COATED RETRIEVER can also be solid black. It follows, therefore, that your Poodle should be either black or chocolate in color to do the clips justice.

The clip that apes the oldest of the Retriever breeds, the CURLY-COATED, is simple. Merely clip the head and muzzle close and trim the legs, body, neck and tail to support an even and fairly close curl all over. Ears should be trimmed to within about an inch of the hair base. Allow some of the longer curl to continue from the top of the neck over the rear portion of the skull.

For the AMERICAN WATER SPANIEL CLIP, clean the face and skull closely and also trim closely under the chin and the top, under-section of the neck. Clip the hair over the body so that the curl is longer than in the Retriever clip. The legs should be trimmed to resemble a Setter's, with longer hair (feather) allowed to grow on the back of the leg while the rest of the leg is cut close. The tail, too, should have feathering, and the hair on the ears should be full and combed out, then shaped fairly round at the base.

The American Water Spaniel Clip

The Irish Water Spaniel Clip

The IRISH WATER SPANIEL more closely resembles the Poodle than do the other two Sporting Dogs. Here we clean the muzzle and cheeks closely, but allow the skull hair to form a topknot which is not overhigh or full and begins level with the dog's eyes. The coat all over the body is left about an inch and a half long so that it will curl. The hair on the legs is left longer than on the body so that they appear full and curly coated. The tail is clipped close to form a "rat-tail." Ear hair is left full as with the American Spaniel, combed out, and the bottom line trimmed to roundness.

For the large Standard Poodle there are a few mimic clips in the Working Group of canines. The KOMONDOR disguise is very easy to accomplish. Simply allow the Poodle coat to grow naturally, comb it out all over. Use a white colored Standard Poodle and you will have a very close approximation to the Komondor. By going a step further and allowing the coat to gain great profuseness your Standard can appear very

The Old English Sheepdog Clip

much like an OLD ENGLISH SHEEPDOG particularly if he is grey in color. THE HUNGARIAN PULIK can be aped by a large Miniature or small Standard Poodle that is a little long in body and either black, grey, or white. Again we have a Poodle masquerade that is more a matter of hair growth and grooming than clipping.

The GIANT SCHNAUZER CLIP has been discussed previously. The difficulty with this clip is that the ears of the Schnauzer are cropped. To simulate the natural ear, trim the ear hair rather close and scissor away all long ends. Similar to the Schnauzer trim is that of the BRIARD. Again we have a dog with a long tail, so simply allow as much feather as can be kept combed straight down on the Poodle's shorter tail. The neck, in the Briard clip, should not be shorn as closely as in the Schnauzer clip and the hair on the hind legs must be more profuse. All solid colors are permissable in the Briard except white. For all intents and purposes, a clip to mimic the BOUVIER

The Giant Schnauzer or Bouvier Clip

The Briard Clip

DES FLANDRES would be the same as the Giant Schnauzer clip. Chocolate Poodles should not be used in these clips. Incidentally, though the Schnauzer clip was described under Terrier clips, the Standard Schnauzer, like its big brother, the Giant Schnauzer, has been, for the last several years, shown in the A.K.C. designated Working Group.

Toy Poodles can wear the disguise of three other tiny dogs in their Toy group, the MALTESE (a breed which, some authorities claim, was utilized in early breedings to bring down the size of the Poodle to the Toy category), the AFFEN-PINSCHER, and the YORKSHIRE TERRIER, the latter a true Toy dog despite its name.

The Yorkshire's erect ears may tend to give your Poodle's disguise away. But his coat can certainly be trained to resemble the Yorkie's. Here again we have a disguise that is more a matter of growth and grooming than of clipping. In developing the Yorkie coat on your Poodle be careful that you don't allow it to become corded.

The Yorkshire Terrier Clip

The AFFENPINSCHER also has erect ears, cropped and trained to erectness. Other than this, and the fact that its tail is cropped very close, the Toy Poodle can fairly well be made to approach its appearance. Clip the hair on the legs in much the same pattern as in the Terrier clips but with a little less squareness in the appearance of the finished clip. The closest to the natural coat color would be a grey; a Maltese is always white.

The Affenpinscher Clip

A FEW SPECIAL GROOMING HINTS

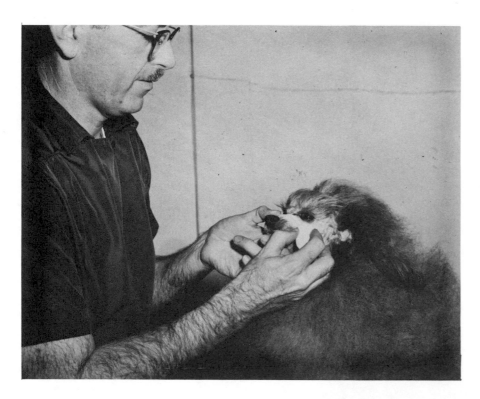

Commercial products are available that will remove the tear-stains that mar the hair below the Poodle's eyes.

A Miniature wearing "Papillotte" wrappings and sporting a Continental Clip (with a very prominent hip pompon) having its mane brushed to fullness.

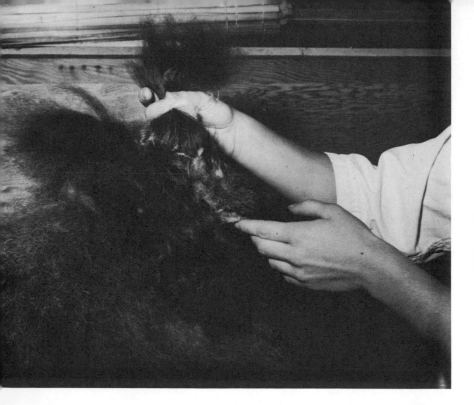

First gather the
topknot hair in your hand
after you have separated the
hair of the crown into two sections.

Spray with coat
conditioner, use cotton
wrap around hair, and wrap
piece of plastic around both
hair and cotton.

78

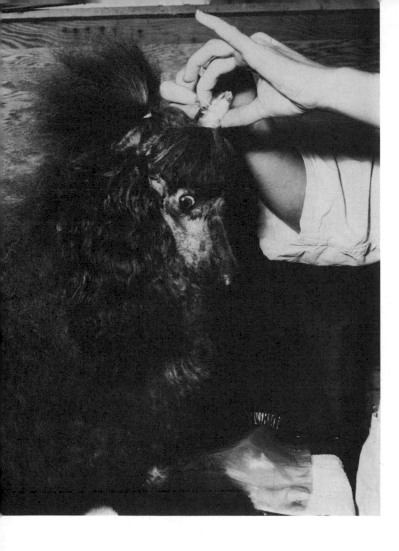

Fold hair-encased
plastic over twice and
tie it down with a rubber band.

Repeat same treatment
with ears. Run comb to where
ear ends so that only hair, and no ear,
leather is caught in rubber band.

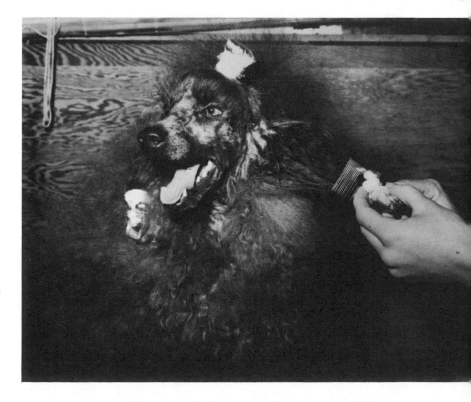

If you have read as far as this you, too, can have well groomed and clipped Poodles like these chic specimens of the finest breed in Dogdom.